COUNTING

IN THE CITY

Please visit our web site at: www.garethstevens.com
For a free color catalog describing our list of high-quality books,
call 1-800-542-2595 (USA) or 1-800-387-3178 (Canada).

Library of Congress Cataloging-in-Publication Data

Sharp, Jean.
    Counting in the city / Jean Sharp. — North American ed.
        p. cm. — (Math in our world)
    ISBN-13: 978-0-8368-8468-5 (lib. bdg.)
    ISBN-10: 0-8368-8468-X (lib. bdg.)
    ISBN-13: 978-0-8368-8477-7 (softcover)
    ISBN-10: 0-8368-8477-9 (softcover)
    1. Counting—Juvenile literature. 2. City and town life—
Juvenile literature. I. Title.
    QA113.S52   2008
    513.2'11—dc22   2007017944

This edition first published in 2008 by
Weekly Reader® Books
An imprint of Gareth Stevens Publishing
1 Reader's Digest Road
Pleasantville, NY 10570-7000   USA

Copyright © 2008 by Gareth Stevens, Inc.

Managing editor: Dorothy L. Gibbs
Art direction: Tammy West
Illustrations: Lorin Walter

Printed in the United States of America

1 2 3 4 5 6 7 8 9 11 10 09 08 07

MATH IN OUR WORLD

COUNTING
IN THE CITY

by Jean Sharp

Illustrations by Lorin Walter

Reading consultant: Susan Nations, M.Ed., author/
literacy coach/consultant in literacy development

Math consultant: Rhea Stewart, M.A., mathematics content specialist

WEEKLY READER®
PUBLISHING

We take a train to the city.

The city is a busy place.
I can count many things.

We walk down the street.
I count 9 buildings.

I count 7 streetlights.

I count 5 yellow taxis.

I count 2 city buses.

We see many people.
I count 3 firefighters.

I count 4 police officers.

I count 10 children.
They are having fun today!

I count 6 teachers.
They watch the children play.

We go to the park.
I count 17 balloons.

I count 13 dogs.
I count 0 cats.

We sit by the pond to eat.
I count 16 boats.

I count 20 ducks.

We see many stores in the city.
I count 12 muffins at the bakery.

I count 11 books at the bookstore.
I love to read books with my mom!

It is night now.
I count 30 lit windows.

I count 24 stars in the sky.

There is I train to take us home.

Counting in the city is fun.

Glossary

bakery

muffin

city

police officer

firefighter

taxi

About the Author

Jean Sharp has authored numerous books and educational software programs for children. A native of Chicago, Illinois, she currently lives with her family in Minneapolis, Minnesota.